The Chur
Bromyard Rural

Avenbury
Chvrch.
Edward Bvrrow
1897

An Informal Guide

By
D. M. Annett

First published by D M Annett in 1987

Revised Edition
The Bromyard & District Local History Society
2003

ISBN 0 9502068 9 X

Set in Times and printed in Great Britain by
Orphans Press, Leominster, Herefordshire

Front Cover Illustration
Evesbatch Church
Back Cover Illustration
Hassocks in St Peter's, Bromyard depicting the Deanery Churches
Designs by Peter Mesdag

Other publications of the Bromyard & District Local History Society:

* *Bromyard: A Local History* (1970)
* *Bromyard Parish Registers* by E D Pearson (1974)
* *Bromyard: The Day Before Yesterday.* A book of photographs (1979)
Whitbourne: A Bishop's Manor by P Williams (1979)
* *Little Cowarne: A Herefordshire Village* by J Hopkinson (1983)
Herefordshire Under Arms by C Hopkinson (1985)
Bromyard: Minster, Manor And Town by P Williams (1987)
A Pocketful of Hops. Hop Growing in the Bromyard Area (1988)
Bromyard: Round And About by D Waller (1991)
Two Churches: Two Communities. St Peter's Bromyard and St James's Stanford Bishop
by E D Pearson (1993)
A History of Bredenbury and its Landed Estate by Jennifer Weale (1997)
Avenbury and the ruined church of St Mary by P Williams (2000)
Where Have All The Courts Gone? A monograph by J Hopkinson (2003)

* OUT OF PRINT

ACKNOWLEDGEMENTS

In 1987, David M Annett produced for the Herefordshire Historic Churches Trust his excellent pamphlet *An Informal Guide To The Parish Churches Of The Bromyard Deanery.*

Mr Annett has now revised and updated the text, and the Bromyard and District Local History Society wish to thank him warmly for his generous offer of publication rights for the benefit of the Society.

The book is enhanced by colour illustrations for each church, for which we are largely indebted to Howard Painter (HFJP) who has given freely of his time and skill. We must also thank John Leonard (JL) for the use of his photographs. The caption to each illustration identifies the photographer by his initials. The map on the inside covers was drawn by Geoff Gwatkin of Ross-on-Wye. Four watercolours from the Pilley Collection (PC) were photographed by Charles Hopkinson and are reproduced with the kind permission of the Herefordshire Libraries and Information Service. Three watercolours on pages 20, 26 and 44 were photographed by Richard Percy and are reproduced with the kind permission of Peter Stokes (PS)

The publication has been supported by financial aid from the Marc Fitch Fund and by the Horace Moore Charitable Trust to whom we are most grateful. Without their help and encouragement this book could not have been produced in colour at such an attractive price. We also wish to thank Orphans Press for their help and co-operation with the final stages of the book.

On behalf of the Publications Sub-Committee,
Marnie Caine
Stephen Guest
Peter Mesdag

St. Mary the Virgin, Bishop's Frome, looking through the lych gate. HFJP

PREFACE

This small book is a revision and enlargement of the original of 1987, which has long been out of print.

It is not intended to give a detailed architectural description of the buildings concerned; this is done authoritatively in the Herefordshire volume of Pevsner's *Buildings of England*. Nor is it intended to give a comprehensive account of the history, architecture and contents of each church; for this one should turn to John Leonard's *Churches of Herefordshire and their Treasures*, and also to the admirable booklets and leaflets which are available in some of the churches. The Deanery is particularly fortunate in the excellent series of parish histories published by the Bromyard and District Local History Society; these are noted in the suggestions for further reading and reference at the end. It may well be asked what then does this book set out to do? The answer is to give a personal and subjective response to each of the churches in the area in the hope that this may stimulate others to visit them and form their own views. The opinions and prejudices expressed are my own, and readers are welcome to disagree with them. If however I have been guilty of any factual errors or blatant omissions, I should be grateful for correction. I have tried to avoid technical terms whenever possible; the few which could not conveniently be dispensed with are explained in the short Glossary at the end.

Newland 2003   D. M. ANNETT

The incised figure of a knight from the ruined church at Avenbury now in St. Peter's Bromyard.

Archaeologia on Miscellaneous Tracts relating to Antiquity (London 1845), 267.

The Bromyard Bushel is in St. Peter's Bromyard.   HFJP

INTRODUCTION

Most of the churches of the Bromyard Deanery may appear at first sight to be lacking in distinction. Not one of them – with the possible exception of Castle Frome, and that only for its font – would rate a place in the County "Top Ten". However, unassuming as they are, there is hardly one that is not worth the attention of a sympathetic visitor, whether for its situation, for some object of interest which it contains, or just for its appealing rustic simplicity.

There are twenty-three churches in the Deanery in present use, though some, like Grendon Bishop, are used infrequently. In addition to these, one is secularised (Tedstone Wafre), one disused (Moreton Jeffries) and two in ruins (Avenbury and Wacton). Then there are the two chapels at Brockhampton, which have never been parochial. The chapel of ease at Linley Green is mentioned at the end of the article on Stanford Bishop.

Anyone visiting these churches will be struck by three characteristics – isolation, simplicity, and the effects of Victorian restoration.

Isolation and simplicity
Most of the churches are in isolated situations – often in the middle of a field, with a farmhouse for company – rather than in the centre of a compact

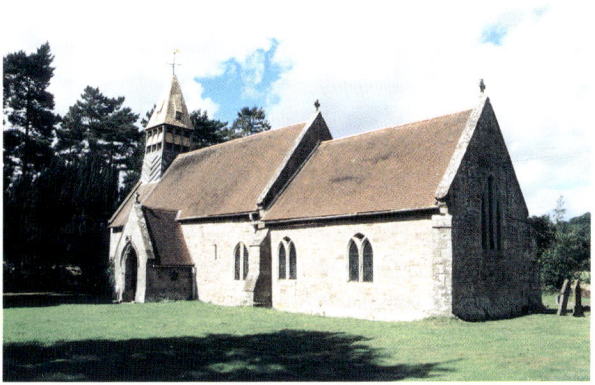

St. Luke's Ullingswick is typical of the small often isolated churches of the Deanery.　　　HFJP

village as is usual in most other parts of England. The reason for this is not necessarily that villages which once existed have disappeared – though this has happened in some cases – but often derives from the early pattern of settlement in this part of Herefordshire, where a parish generally consisted, not of a village centre with its hinterland of fields and woods, but of an area dotted with farms and cottages, the church being found either in the centre of the parish, or adjoining the largest farmhouse or the manor house if there is one.

The churches are usually small and simple, for although the parishes are large, the populations are not. This has of course led to present difficulties of staffing and maintenance, and the old days when each parish had a resident parson are gone forever. Some Herefordshire priests nowadays have responsibility for six or even more churches and parishes, and many churches are kept open by the sentiment and loyalty of a handful of parishioners, where financial and administrative sense would demand their closure. It is indeed surprising how few of these lonely little churches have been closed or made redundant, and equally surprising that almost all of them are open to welcome the chance visitor.

The typical local church consists only of a nave and chancel, with at the west end either a bell-turret, usually supported on a massive timber sub-structure, or a solid stone tower capped with a pyramidal roof. Only four of the churches can boast a side-aisle, and of these only two (Bromyard and Much Cowarne) are medieval. There is not a clerestory in the Deanery. Most of the churches date back at least to the 11th or 12th century, and much of the structure of the walls is usually still Norman; the early date of the foundation of the church is often made clear by the survival of a tiny round-headed window or a crudely but vigorously carved doorway. Another indication of Norman work is the use of the curious spongy-looking stone called tufa (see Glossary).

The exterior of the church may be pleasantly weathered, but on going inside one is often disappointed to find a bland lack of character which has been brought about by two periods of destruction. The first was in the 16th century (after the Reformation) and the 17th (during the Commonwealth) when the wall-paintings were obliterated with whitewash on which texts were painted, the stained-glass smashed, and the Rood destroyed, often with its supporting screen and loft. (To see what these sometimes looked like, one should visit the remote little Black Mountain churches of St. Margaret's and Partrishow, where wonderful lofts have survived.) The second period, in the 19th century, brings us to the third characteristic.

Victorian restoration

It might be expected that in view of the isolation of the churches and the sparseness of the population, they would have escaped the excesses of Victorian restoration. Unfortunately this is not the case, and however small the community, money was found at some time in the 19th century to repair, restore or rebuild the church. After the general apathy and neglect of the 18th century many of the churches must have been in a state of grievous disrepair, but unfortunately the Victorian architects were not satisfied with making the buildings structurally sound while retaining their ancient features and atmosphere; instead they too often swept away old work, on the grounds that it was decayed or inappropriate, and replaced it with something com-

Neo-Norman arches in Bishop's Frome Church.   HFJP

pletely new, the result being, not a restoration of the church as it was, but an "improved" reconstruction as the architect thought it ought to be. With this in mind they destroyed the western gallery where the choir used to sing, accompanied by a village band or a barrel organ, replacing it with choir-stalls for a robed choir in the chancel, in mistaken imitation of cathedral practice, and installing a new pipe organ; this added further to the congestion in the chancel, often blocking a window. All too frequently they also relegated the fine 18th- and early 19th-century wall-monuments to a place of obscurity under the tower. The enclosed box-pews were removed, as was the three-decker pulpit – though these have survived at Moreton Jeffries. Sometimes the old church was rejected altogether as being beyond repair or beneath contempt, and a completely new one built in its place. The old one was demolished entirely (as at Bredenbury and Collington) or unroofed and left in ruins nearby (as at Edvin Loach and Tedstone Wafre).

Apart from the destruction of old buildings and fittings, the Victorian architects had a passion for stripping the plaster from the internal walls. In medieval times these, if built of rough unsquared stones, were plastered and then covered with paintings which, together with the stained-glass windows, provided religious "visual aids" for a largely illiterate congregation. By removing the plaster the Victorians did great damage in two ways. First, they exposed rough rubble stone-work which was never intended to be seen, and which, because of the dark colour of much local stone, often gives a

The font at Castle Frome, one of the masterpieces of the Herefordshire school of sculpture.

gloomy air to the interiors. Secondly, and much more seriously, with the plaster they destroyed the hidden wall-paintings, which modern techniques could have restored to view by removing the covering coats of whitewash. To see what has been lost, one must visit the Old Church at Kempley, near Much Marcle but just over the Gloucestershire border, where almost the whole interior of the little Norman church is covered with wonderful medieval paintings, recently restored. It would be wrong to pretend that all or any of our local churches would have equalled Kempley, but most of them would probably have had on their walls at least a large figure of St. Christopher opposite the door and a "doom" over the chancel arch (these were vivid and attention-gripping pictures of the Last Judgment, with the blessed on one side being led off to the Heavenly Mansions, and the damned on the other being dragged away by gleeful devils to the Jaws of Hell). Too few churches in the Deanery have retained their plastered walls, and I do not think that a scrap of medieval painting remains; many churches would be greatly improved and lightened if the plaster were replaced.

INTRODUCTION

As a footnote to all this, an interesting light is thrown on the methods of some Victorian restorers by a personal letter from Mrs. E. Wright, whose father, Preb. F. Simcox Lea, was Rector of Tedstone Delamere from 1873 to 1893.

"When my father came there (Tedstone), he was horrified to find that when Gilbert Scott, the architect, restored the church and did away with the gallery, he let all the carved oak be used for shelves in the Rectory coach-house and saddle-room, and even for door-posts for the open cow-shed in the Rectory field. My father had every bit removed, and he gave it all to Mr. Onslow, the Rector of Upper Sapey, who was doing something then to his parish church.... Another crime of the architect was that he used the memorial stone slabs in the church floor to cover the new heating pipes, and then hid the stones under common tiles."

(This oak was presumably used for the pulpit and panelling in the chancel of Upper Sapey, installed at about this time.) Since every church to be mentioned bears the scars of Victorian restoration to a greater or lesser degree, the abbreviation "VR" has been used when referring to it.

When visiting one of these churches today, one should think back to what it was like in previous centuries, looking for indications of the past which have survived, and trying to understand how the changes in the structure and furnishings of the church – sometimes over a period of 800 years – reflect the changes in religious practices, in social life and in artistic taste.

Finally, please spare a grateful thought for the small community of people and their parish priest, who by their devotion, their efforts and their generosity have maintained each of these buildings as a House of God and a focus for the life of the parochial community.

Re-used oak panelling from Tedstone Delamere on the pulpit in St. Michael's Upper Sapey. HFJP

LIST OF CHURCHES

Acton Beauchamp
Avenbury
Bishop's Frome
Bredenbury
Brockhampton
Bromyard
Castle Frome
Collington
Cowarne, Little
Cowarne, Much
Edvin Loach
Edwyn Ralph
Evesbatch
Frome's Hill

Grendon Bishop
Moreton Jeffries
Ocle Pychard
Pencombe
Stanford Bishop
Stoke Lacy
Tedstone Delamere
Tedstone Wafre
Thornbury
Ullingswick
Upper Sapey
Wacton
Whitbourne
Wolferlow

The bell chamber at St. Peter's Bromyard circa 1968. A. Wall and C. Wall with D. Hinksman (front) the Tower captain. B&DLHS

5

JL

Although St. Giles was a popular medieval saint, little is known for certain about his life. According to legend he lived for some years as a hermit in a forest, attended by a hind; later, he became abbot of a monastery in southern France. He is usually shown – though not here at Acton Beauchamp – as an abbot holding a crozier, with a hind at his feet.

In the secluded and beautiful valley of the upper Frome, the church is surprisingly placed on the steep slope of a hill which is crowned by the fine Georgian red-brick Church House Farm, with its magnificent farm buildings and walls, giving from below almost the appearance of a castle. The church is unique in the Deanery in being in the Classical style, having been rebuilt about 1820 with large round-headed windows filled with clear glass. One says "style", but in fact the building could hardly be plainer, with plastered walls and ceilings, and no decoration of any kind.

All that remains from the medieval building is the west tower, with the usual pyramidal roof, a Norman arch to the south door with one capital carved with three delightful heads, a simple 15th-century font, and – most surprising of all – a very fine but mutilated slab covered with rich Anglo-Saxon carving

Anglo-Saxon carving set in the south wall of the tower.
JL

The Classical interior; note the commandment boards still in place on the east wall. HFJP

(9th century?). At some time it has been set into the south wall of the tower as a lintel for the door, and a large slice unfortunately carved out of it to give more headroom.

Inside the church is a wall monument which declares, with a fine disregard for conventional spelling, "The remains of Henry Brace where hear interred May 9th 1773 aged 72 years". The two boards painted with the Ten Commandments are still in their original place (though repainted) on the east wall above the altar; these together with the Lord's Prayer and the Creed were made obligatory in the reign of Elizabeth I, but few remain *in situ* nowadays.

The wall monument to Henry Brace. HFJP

7

What now remains of the tower of this church. HFJP

From the nearest lane hardly anything can now be seen of the ruined church of Avenbury among its clump of trees. Having made one's way to it along an over-grown path, one wonders not so much why the church was abandoned as why it was ever built in this empty and beautiful part of the Frome valley, a mile or so south of Bromyard. However the thickly populated graveyard indicates that it was once the centre of a sizeable parish community, and a full account of the place can be found in Phyllis Williams's history of the parish. Services were held here until the 1930s, but now all that remains is the usual solid western tower and the walls of the chancel – roofless and masked in ivy and elder, but still showing traces of two little Norman windows. The drawing on the title page of this book shows the church as it was in 1897; now it is a sad and rather sinister place. (The memorial slab bearing the "incised figure of a knight" men-tioned in the guide-books has been removed to Bromyard Church, see page iv, and other relics are at Bishop's Frome.)

BISHOP'S FROME - St. Mary the Virgin

The tower is genuine 14th-century work, but as one approaches the church one's suspicions are aroused, and in fact all the rest of it was rebuilt in 1847 (chancel) and 1861 (nave and aisle) in mock-Norman style by F. R. Kempson of Hereford. He built, rebuilt and restored a large number of churches all over the county – five in this Deanery alone. He usually worked in a Victorian Gothic style, in which his *chef d'oeuvre* is the City Library in Broad Street, Hereford. At Bishop's Frome he unusually tried his hand at neo-Norman and it seems to have gone to his head. Pevsner severely describes his work here as "terribly pretentious and not even archaeologically correct". A more sympathetic critic might say that he was developing the original medieval styles in a creative and imaginative way – but this would take a considerable effort of generosity, for Kempson's work here, particularly in the north arcade, (see page 2) is undeniably extravagant and indigestible. The south porch provides an instructive comparison; the outer arch is Kempson having fun with his mock-Norman, while the inner doorway is a plain and dignified example of the real thing, 700 years older. He also allowed the Norman chancel arch to survive, filled with a mainly 15th-century wooden screen, and there are two mysterious stones with elaborate 12th-century carving set into the exterior south wall of the chancel, on either side of the priest's door.

Inside the church there are many interesting things to see. The font is a huge plain lead-lined bowl of red sandstone (probably 12th-century) on a modern base. In a recess in the south wall of the nave is the fine stone figure of a knight (13th-century). His legs are crossed, he wears a chain-mail head-dress, and he appears to be drawing his sword. The chancel is carpeted wall-to-wall in modern domestic style, but some fine ledger-stones have been lifted from the floor and ranged round the walls so that they can still be seen. The east window is filled with unusual pictorial glass which presumably dates from the 1847 restoration, though it looks earlier.

This screen came originally from Avenbury Church.   HFJP

In 1995 a chapel was formed at the end of the north aisle, using some partly medieval screen-work and some handsome 18th-century communion rails; both of these came originally from Avenbury Church when it was closed in 1931, then spent 50 years in Munderfield Chapel, which in turn closed in 1980; one hopes that this is their final resting place. Set into the east wall is a most unusual painted wooden memorial to Margery Pychard (d.1598) and her husband George de la Downes. They are shown kneeling on either side of a prayer

F. R. Kempson's interior.   JL

The 13th-century effigy of a knight.   HFJP

desk surrounded by a flurry of inscriptions in English and Latin which have been thoughtfully transcribed and translated on a framed card hanging on the wall nearby.

The old parish chest, dating probably from about 1600, has had one of its locks hacked out. (Parish chests had three locks with different keys; the vicar and two churchwardens had one each, so that the chest could be opened only when all three were present.)

The churchyard – or at least the south side of it – is particularly pleasant because for once the 18th- and early 19th-century headstones and tomb-chests have not been uprooted, – and a fine collection they are. From the eastern gate a short avenue of aged and distorted limes, reputedly planted in 1858, leads down to the river Frome; one wonders why.

The old parish chest showing the hacked out lock. HFJP

HFJP

The church was built on a new site in 1876/7, the old church having stood on what is now the lawn in front of Bredenbury Court – where it doubtless blocked the fine view towards the Malverns from the windows of the house. A photograph of it dated 1874 hanging in the new church suggests that it was an undistinguished building of the usual local type, but in too good a condition to justify its demolition (it was pulled down in 1876). The present St. Andrew's is a typical small Victorian church, carefully Gothic, handsomely appointed, embellished with an elaborately carved reredos and pulpit, and darkened by a complete set of 19th-century stained glass windows by various designers, but mostly of mediocre quality. When this new church was built to serve the combined parishes of Bredenbury and Wacton, both old churches were demolished. A window and some mural tablets from the old Bredenbury Church were moved to the new one, and some relics from Wacton are also preserved there (see Wacton) – though "preserved" is hardly the right word for the treatment of the font.

The elaborately carved pulpit.   HFJP

BROCKHAMPTON - The Old Chapel

(The two chapels at Brockhampton should properly be excluded from this survey, since they have never been parish churches, but as they are seen by many visitors to Lower Brockhampton, some notes may be helpful).

The Old Chapel: The old chapel next to the moated medieval manor-house of Lower Brockhampton is now abandoned and roofless. It is a small and simple building, with no structural division between nave and chancel. The walls are obviously Norman in origin, since they are largely built of tufa, but the arches of the doorway and windows are all pointed, and therefore later. At the west end is a battered

The east window.   HFJP

font, and in the floor at the east end some 17th- to 18th-century ledger-stones to Barnebys (the lords of the manor) and their Lechmere relatives. The chapel became disused after the new chapel was built at the top of the park near the new Georgian house, and presumably fell into disrepair or was used as a farm building. Perhaps the mysterious holes in the walls were inserted at this time to provide ventilation.

The font.   HFJP

13

The new chapel.   HFJP

The New Chapel: The new chapel is a miniature grey stone church complete with pinnacled tower, standing romantically half-hidden by yews and rhodo-dendrons in the park of Brockhampton House. The architect was George Byfield, whose drawings are dated 1798/9, though the church was not conse-crated until 1810. It is a charming early "Gothic revival" building, designed with an eye to scenic effect; on the side away from the road there are no win-dows and no battlemented parapets. Inside, the original fittings remain almost untouched. The pews are arranged in tiers facing each other as in a college chapel; there is a gallery (for the servants and estate workers) and a two-deck-er pulpit. The lower part of the east wall is covered with very handsome mosa-ic work by Powell (cp. Whitbourne); set in the middle of the reredos is, sur-prisingly, a small Russian icon painted by Ivan Malyshev of the Sergiev Monastery in 1874. This was given by Colonel Lutley, the last Lord of the Manor, who bequeathed the whole estate to the National Trust in 1947. On the walls is a fine collection of memorial tablets to Barnebys, Lutleys and their relations, spanning 150 years. There are also a number of smaller tablets to faithful estate workers – a wagoner, a coachman and others.

In the south-west corner, half-hidden by the gallery, is a remarkable window with a strange history. It is painted, not stained, glass, and was made by W. R. Eginton, presumably in 1810, to fill the east window. It was inspired by a "Transfiguration" by Raphael in the Vatican, but Eginton curiously trans-formed it into a "Resurrection" by adding the marks of the Passion on Christ's hands and feet. By the 1880s painted glass had become unfashionable, and the window was replaced by the present one by Powell in very much more subdued colours and less dramatic style; it represents Faith, Charity and Hope (in that order), and was also inspired by paintings by Raphael. Eginton's glass was removed to the window in the south-west corner, but since this has only two lights, the right-hand panel of the original had to be discarded. A good deal of

The east end - note the Russian icon set in the reredos.　　　　HFJP

other damage was done to the glass in the process of moving it. Plans are afoot for restoring it, and one hopes that this will be possible, for it is a striking and unusual possession. The other windows in the chapel are all by Powell, mostly designed by two pioneer female stained-glass designers, Mary Lowndes and Ada Currey, the latter of whom also designed the figure of Christ in mosaic which dominates the apse of the church at Hoarwithy. (All the information about these windows is the result of recent research by Dennis Hadley and David Boddington, recorded in Journal 24 (2002) of the Bromyard and District Local History Society.)

The chapel is now served from Bromyard Parish Church, and services are held in it regularly. Unfortunately owing to vandalism and thefts it has to be kept locked; anyone wishing to visit it should apply to the vicar of Bromyard or Dr. David Boddington.

The west end showing the gallery and the pews facing each other across the aisle.　　　　HFJP

BROMYARD - St. Peter

Although the massive tower, with its striking and unusual round turret, is a dominant feature of the town in views from the north and east, the church makes no visual impact on the town itself, being secluded on the northern edge, away from the main streets. It is a large cruciform building, but it is

HFJP

less impressive than it might be, both externally and internally, owing to the absence of a clerestory. Lacking this source of light, the interior of the nave would have been very dark, were it not for the flat white plaster ceilings, which, fortunately and surprisingly, survived the VR. Many medieval churches were probably ceiled in this way in the 18th century, but the Victorians generally removed the ceilings to expose the roof timbers, just as they stripped the plaster from the walls to expose the stonework.

Bromyard was an important religious centre in Saxon times, with a "minster" church, but of this virtually nothing has survived. There are however considerable remains of the Norman church which followed it – most notably two very fine doorways, one on the north and the other on the south, both having been reset in the new outer walls when the aisles were built. That on the south has had a pointed arch cut through its tympanum (possibly at the same time): above it is a little carved figure of St. Peter with his keys, and a consecration cross, both possibly relics of the Saxon church. Inside, one of the first things to meet one's eyes is a tub-shaped Norman font, with rich, if crude, carved decoration. The two lofty nave arcades are identical at first glance, but the northern one is about 40 years later, as can be seen from the carved foliage which has

begun to appear on the capitals, whereas those on the south are carved with the plainer trumpet shapes characteristic of Norman work. The pillars of the arcades were heightened in 1805. This sounds an unusual operation, but the same thing had been done in Ross-on-Wye Church in 1743. The plaster ceilings must have been put in at the same time.

In the chancel are a number of fine 18th-century mural tablets with ele-

St. Peter with his keys, over the south door. HFJP

gant and flattering inscriptions. The locality was blessed with some admirable women, to judge from the tributes to Betty Barneby (d. 1785) and Laetitia Pauncefort (d. 1753) whose epitaph ends: "Reader, if thou knowest her worth, weep thy own loss: if not, weep that thou didst not know her". The striking east and west windows, both designed by A. K. Nicholson, were installed in the 1930s. The east window illustrates Christ's words "I am the vine: ye are the branches" combining them with the Te Deum. The west window commemorates two musical families, and shows St. Cecilia, patron saint of music, surrounded by an angelic choir, with some famous English musicians below. Hidden away in an obscure position on the floor in the north-west corner of the north aisle is the fine

The Te Deum window at the east end above the altar. HFJP

tomb-slab with an incised figure of a knight (see page iv) removed from the church at Avenbury after it was abandoned in the 1930s. Sitting disconsolately not far from it is the "Bromyard Bushell" – (see page iv) a massive bowl of bell-metal standing on four feet, with an inscription saying that it is a standard bushel authorised by Act of Parliament in 1670. (There are plans to move both these handsome and interesting objects to positions where they can be seen to better advantage.) One strange feature of the church is the number of arched recesses in the walls – six inside and two outside. They were presumably made to contain tombs, but they are all empty now.

The spacious churchyard has been stripped of headstones, which are ranged along the walls, but fortunately some fine early 19th-century tomb-chests of a variety of designs have been left *in situ.*

Chairs replaced pews in the nave in 2002. HFJP

CASTLE FROME - St. Michael

The church stands pleasantly above the road, backed by a wood which hides the scanty remains of the castle. There used to be a beautiful view westward to the Welsh hills, but in recent years the foreground has been filled with the buildings of an agricultural/commercial firm – which presumably did not need planning permission. As usual, a large farmhouse stands nearby, but there is no village. VR here for once deserves praise: the half-timbered porch and bell-turret are attractive and appropriate additions – but unfortunately the plaster was scraped from the interior walls. Though almost entirely Norman, the church is unusually lofty and spacious. It contains three remarkable objects: first, the superb 12th-century font, one of the masterpieces of the Herefordshire School of sculptors (see page 3), and suf-

The half-timbered porch and bell turret. HFJP

The 17th-century monument to a cavalier and his wife. HFJP

18

CASTLE FROME - St. Michael

ficiently notable to have been removed to London for the great Romanesque Exhibition of 1984: second, the splendid and wonderfully-preserved 17th-century monument to a cavalier and his wife, with their children ranged round the sides: and thirdly – tucked away inaccessibly at the foot of a window in the chancel – the tiny carved figure of a knight, holding his heart in his hands and apparently smiling. This may commemorate a heart-burial; if a crusading knight died in Palestine, his heart was sometimes preserved and

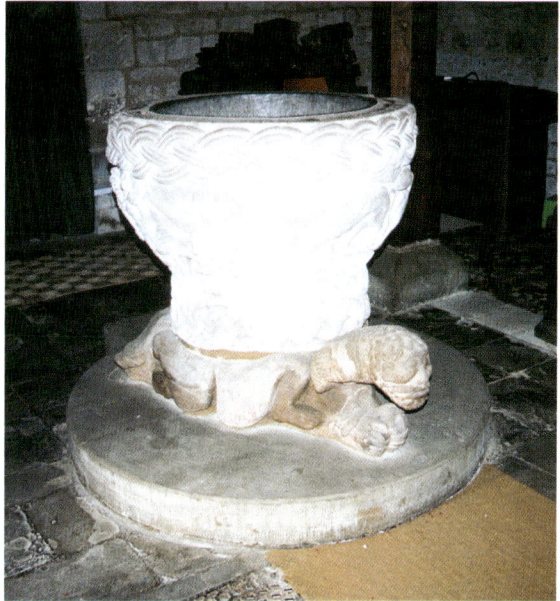

The 12th-century font.   HFJP

sent home for burial. In the churchyard is a vast and ancient yew. There is also near the gate a simple memorial stone with this inscription "In loving and grateful memory of John Cave Pudge who was born at Frogend on 11th October 1898 and died there 29th March 1969" – a moving tribute to the stability of the countryside. How many of us can expect to die in the house in which we were born 70 years before?

A crusading knight holding his heart.   HFJP

The present church built in 1856. HFJP

In 1352 the two parishes of Great and Little Collington were so depopulated by plague that the inhabitants petitioned the Bishop to unite the parishes. This was done, and as Little Collington Church (All Saints) was in better condition and more suitable, this became the parish church. It stood near Church House Farm - about half a mile east of the main road. All that is left there now is a chest tomb with other memorial stones stacked against it; the early watercolour below shows the church.

The Church of Great Collington was presumably demolished or allowed to fall into dereliction and its site is now unknown. The present church in its well-kept churchyard is entirely a building of 1856, and the only material evidence of an earlier church is the font - octagonal with very simple carved arches on the sides. One cannot say more than that it is medieval; it has lost its base and stands knee-high - which must be awkward for baptisms.

Little Collington Church, demolished in the nineteenth century, with the chest tomb still in situ, that marks the site of the churchyard, on the right. PS

COWARNE, LITTLE - St. Guthlac

What we see is a complete rebuilding of the church by Kempson in 1869, though he retained or reset various windows and doors from the old church, including the usual tiny Norman window in the chancel. (This work is described in detail in the excellent leaflet available in the church.) The bowl of the font is probably 12th-century. A puzzle; the piscina in the south wall of the sanctuary has no drain, while the square aumbry on the north side has one. Was this a muddle by Kempson's mason, which he overlooked? To him is owed the attractive saddle-back tower with its unusual cross-gable. On the north wall of the nave is a splendid millennium wall-hanging illustrating many scenes and activities in the village, worked by a number of ladies of the parish.

In 1992 the church, of which the original dedication – if there ever was one – was lost, was dedicated by the Bishop of Hereford to St. Guthlac, to commemorate the fact that in early times the church was appropriated to St. Guthlac's Priory at Hereford.

The millennium wall-hanging worked by the ladies of the parish. HFJP

21

HFJP

The church is approached through a farmyard, and instead of the modest building one usually finds in such a situation it is a pleasant surprise to be faced with what is, after Bromyard, the grandest church in the Deanery, – and it was even grander before the spire was removed in 1840 after having been struck by lightning, and the north aisle demolished. Moreover, the church has mercifully escaped the usual drastic VR. In the 13th century Much Cowarne was important enough to be granted a charter for a market and a fair, and this explains the size and distinction of the church in what is now a sparsely populated parish. By the 16th century the village had declined, and the demolition of the now unnecessary north aisle may have taken place about this time. Before entering the church (the whereabouts of the key should be ascertained beforehand) walk round the outside. Standing at the foot of the tower you will find that the church is set on a rise, and commands fine views over the water meadows and the recently restored fish ponds. The large and impressive tower seems to have been in danger, at various times, of sliding down into the stream, for it is propped by a strange collection of buttresses of differing shapes and dates. On the north side of the church can be seen the pillars and arches of the original north arcade, with the 13th-century windows and door of the old aisle wall moved back and fitted uncomfortably into the arches.

The 14th-century south arcade.　　HFJP

The pillars and arches of the original north aisle can be seen on the north side of the church.   HFJP

On entering the church one is struck by its height and spaciousness, and the elegance of the lofty south arcade (14th century), the finest piece of architecture in any of the Deanery churches. There are three interesting monuments. The first is the sadly mutilated effigy of a knight, with chain mail headdress and crossed legs like the one at Bishop's Frome. He is said to be Grimbald Pauncefoot, and the remarkable story of how his faithful wife Constance redeemed him from captivity in Tunis by cutting off her hand and sending it as ransom is told in an illuminated account hanging on the wall nearby. As late as the 17th century her effigy was to be seen beside his, with her truncated arm raised, and the amputated hand lying beside her. One wonders whatever can be the explanation of the disappearance of such a remarkable monument. Next to Grimbald is the handsome tomb-chest of Edmund Fox (d. 1617): he and his wife lie on top of it, and their thirteen children are ranged round the sides. Finally, in the chancel is the monument to Sybil Reed (d. 1624), with her recumbent effigy, and four children kneeling behind her. There are three piscinas in the church, showing that there must have been at least three altars. The fine glass in the east window dates from the early part of the 20th century.

The tomb chest of Edmund Fox (d.1617) and his wife.   HFJP

23

The two adjoining parishes of Edvin Loach and Edwyn Ralph obviously share the same first name – which appears as Gedefen or Gedefin in Domesday Book – but recently a spirit of local independence has introduced the more genteel

The round-headed doorway of the old church showing the huge blocks of tufa. HFJP

Edwyn for the western village. Edvin Loach takes its second name from the Norman family of *de Loges*, Edwyn Ralph from a Ralph *de Edefen*, one of the lords of the manor there.

The two churches at Edvin Loach, approached by a gated farm track, stand lonely in a churchyard carpeted with snowdrops in early spring, on top of a hill from which there is a superb view northwards to Clee Hill and south-east to the Malverns. One comes first to the ruins of the old church, which may well date back to pre-Norman times, for much of the masonry is laid in the extraordinary herring-bone pattern generally associated with Saxon work. The simple round-headed doorway and some of the corner stones are formed by huge blocks of tufa (see Tedstone Delamere). At the west end stand the remains of a little tower (16th century?) with timber framings still surviving in the openings. Some years ago the ruins were taken into the care of English Heritage. Two bells from the old church, one dated 1629 and the other of 14th-century date, formerly stood on the floor of the new church, together with a third bell of 1674 which probably came from Tedstone Wafre old church. Sad to relate, all three were stolen in 1998.

The herring-bone pattern of the masonry is generally associated with Saxon work. HFJP

The new church, a few yards to the west, was designed by the noted Victorian architect Sir George Gilbert Scott, and built in 1860, at the expense of the Higginson/Barneby family of nearby Saltmarshe Castle (demolished in 1953). It is an imposing building, with a three-sided apse at the east end and a tower at the west with a stone spire visible for miles around. Inside the church, the tower is rather oddly supported on two stout columns. At the time when the new church was built, the old church was dilapidated but still roofed. One can only wish that instead of building a new church, the benefactors had spent their money on restoring the old one. Small as it is, it would have been large enough for the needs of the parish which has probably never had more than the present eleven dwellings.

The interior of the new church.   HFJP

25

EDWYN RALPH - St. Michael

(For an explanation of the name of the parish, see Edvin Loach)

HFJP

The church is approached through a dark grove of yews, and has a massive tower like that of nearby Thornbury, crowned by a curious combination of pyramid-roof and spirelet. The south door is interesting for two reasons. Although it carries typical Norman decoration, the arch is pointed: one therefore assumes that it was rebuilt in the 13th century or later, using the stones of the original round Norman arch. Built into the east jamb is a rare survival – a stoup, or stone bowl for holy water, in which the worshippers could dip their fingers and cross themselves before entering the church. Every church had at least one of these, but most were destroyed at the Reformation.

The interior is a surprise – a single long chamber with no chancel arch or screen. The cream-painted walls and the white ceiling, showing up the elaborate pattern of the trussed rafter roof, produce an agreeably light effect. The only division between nave and chancel is another rare survival – the rood beam, on which originally stood the rood (crucifix) with attendant figures of the

This 19th-century watercolour demonstrates how little the church has changed. PS

26

Blessed Virgin and St. John. In the centre of the beam can be seen the sockets in which the three figures were fastened.

The glory – and the shame – of Edwyn Ralph Church is the extraordinary collection of medieval effigies deplorably ban-

The interior showing the rood beam. HFJP

ished to huddled obscurity under the tower. There are seven in all, and they are said to commemorate members of the Edefen family, who took their name from the manor. The earliest (late 13th century) are of a husband and wife, he in armour; then comes a cross-legged knight (early 14th century) with fleur-de-lys on his shield: beside him lie two ladies, presumably his successive wives. There is also a small unattached female figure – a child? All these are "in the round" but there is also a flat slab with the elaborately incised figure of a lady (c. 1325) surrounded by an inscription identifying her as Maud de Edefen, and promising sixty days of pardon to those saying a "paternoster" and an "ave" for her. There can be few parish churches in the county which possess such a

magnificent collection of medieval monuments, and one stands aghast that they should – presumably during the inevitable VR – have been relegated to their present shameful position. In the chancel are two arched recess- es surmounted by carved heads (cp. Wolferlow and Upper Sapey) from which some of the figures must have been removed. In 1824 the antiquary Peter Prattinton saw six effigies on the north side of the chancel. One can only hope that some wealthy benefactor might make it pos- sible for these splendid monu- ments to be given the hon- oured position they deserve.

A donations board listing benefactors of the church. HFJP

HFJP

From the road the little church looks charming, squatting neatly like a partridge in its tidy churchyard, with the obligatory yew. Unfortunately VR in 1877 was heavy, and for once no recognisably Norman work survives, except perhaps the extremely simple font, with its delightful Jacobean cover. Only one medieval window remains – small, but of an unusual and pleasing design, with tracery under a round arch, – and this has been copied elsewhere in the church. Hidden away on the west wall and very difficult to see are two robustly and richly carved and painted monuments to members of the Dobyns family, both with sad stories. On the left stands Mrs. Dobyns. She died in 1658 giving birth to the stillborn baby which she holds in her arms. Her epitaph reads:

Her lieth a Mother in our Mother's Wombe
Who to her onely child did prove a Tombe.
Thus Heavens did decree, that she should have
A son, Heire of her Body and her Grave.
Though she a Mother was, she did begin
Strange not till after death for to lye in.
More for to tell you, WHO WHAT here doth lye
Would prove WITH beauty and the best must die.

On the other side is the memorial to Catherine Dobyns, who died at the age of 12 in 1710. Her epitaph reads:

The east window. HFJP

Deare to her parents here doth lye
A maid admired for piety.
Of yeares but Twelve, yet she knew more
of God, than many at threescore.
What meekeness, Goodness, inno-cence
In a sad hour was snacht from hence.
Fate gives but seldome length of days
To plants of such esteeme and praise.
The stars cant suffer such a Birth
To be long sully'd with dull Earth.
What reason have wee then to prize
The dearest object of our Eyes.
Cease wee then from unjust com-plaints,
For Heaven loves such early Saints.

It is hard to forgive the Victorian restorers for removing such wall-monu-ments from their original places, where they could be seen and appreciated, and hiding them away as here, at Whitbourne, and elsewhere. (The epi-taphs have been transcribed here, because in their present position they are not easy to read.) The epitaph of Catherine's father Robert, in contrast to hers, is brief and pithy:

The monument to Mrs. Dobyns who died in childbirth in 1658. HFJP

Here lies a counseller, deny who can,
Who lived and died an honest man.

(This inscription, on a slab in the floor, is partially obliterated, but fortunately was recorded in 1902)

The pew-ends incorporate rough-hewn and primitive carved panels, while the modern screen and pulpit also seem to contain pieces of older work.

The east window is an elaborate example of the work of one of the most famous late Victorian stained glass designers, C. E. Kempe, many of whose windows can be seen in Ledbury Church and Leominster Priory. On opening the door to leave the church, one is greeted by a lovely view to the distant hills.

HFJP

This church has the rare distinction of having been overlooked by Pevsner. It is a pleasant and unassuming little building of 1864 designed by F. R. Kempson in one of his quieter moments. The semicircular apse and tall bell cote give it a touch of individuality.

HFJP

GRENDON BISHOP - St. John the Baptist

Surely the loneliest of all the lonely churches in the Deanery. A farm lane leads from the A44 to Grendon Manor Farm, where the key is kept. From here the church is 300 yards away across the fields, with not even a path leading to it – yet services are still held here once or twice a year. What we see must be at least the third church on the site, for on the south face of the tower is a tiny round-headed window; this, and the tub-shaped font, indicate that there was a Norman building here. But, as we are informed by a tablet inside the church, "This church was rebuilt at the expense of the inhabitants of this parish. The first stone was laid by James Jenks in the year 1786..." Of this "classical" church not a trace remains; what we see is an uninspired Victorian rebuilding (c. 1870) including a pretentious and inappropriate polygonal apse. What is of interest are the monuments. On the walls inside is a handsome and varied collection of mural tablets dating from the 18th and early 19th centuries, some of which must have come from the pre-1786 building – including one erected by the strikingly named Cimbriana Morris to her late husband.

Outside the south door, oddly crowded together between the church wall and a great yew, is a very fine group of early 19th-century monuments, including four chest-tombs. The presence of all these memorials, together with the tablet recording the 1786 rebuilding, is evidence that this now almost derelict little church was once the centre of a sizeable and prosperous community.

These mural tablets must have come from an earlier church. HFJP

HFJP

This humble little church hides behind a large yew, seemingly overawed by the two large Victorian farmhouses nearby, which look as if they had strayed from a prosperous city suburb into rural Herefordshire. This church is no longer used for services, but has been fortunate enough to be adopted by the Churches Conservation Trust, which is now responsible for its maintenance, at no cost to the parish or diocese. From outside one wonders why it was thought worthy of such favoured treatment, but on entering one sees the reason. In spite of VR the church is full of old furnishings – pews which look 17th-century, boards with the Lord`s Prayer and the Creed on the east wall, a heavy screen, into which is built something unique in the deanery – a fine three-decker pulpit – Jacobean, and very grand for such a modest church. The lowest level was occupied by the parish clerk, who led the congregation in the responses and psalms;

These boards carrying the Lord's Prayer and the Creed were spared by the Victorians, but two with the Ten Commandments have disappeared. HFJP from the middle storey the parson prayed and read the lessons, and he ascended to the topmost storey to preach. These were commonplace fittings in churches in the 17th and 18th centuries, but were almost all swept away in 19th-century restorations.

The three-decker pulpit.   HFJP

St. James, Ocle Pychard.   HFJP

The tower is built half inside the nave and half outside – a peculiar arrangement – and is crowned by a small copper-covered spire which has turned a brilliant green, and catches the eye from miles around, for the church is built on high ground, and commands splendid views across to the Black Mountains. The church is basically of 13th- and 14th-century date but was subjected to heavy VR; the scraping of the walls is regrettable, for the dark exposed stone makes parts of the building rather gloomy. The doorway high up in the wall above the pulpit led to the former rood loft across the chancel arch. This would have been approached by a door on the east side of the wall leading to a staircase in the thickness of the wall, but both of these have disappeared, as has the loft and the screen which supported it (see Glossary). There is however a piscina in the south-east corner of the nave showing that an altar stood in front of the screen there, where the modern replacement now stands. A "charity board" hangs in the north-west corner of the nave, and on the west wall are the two "commandments boards" which were originally fixed to the east wall (see Acton Beauchamp). There are two fonts, one dating from the VR and the other a 15th-century one ejected at that time, but brought back in 1939.

The Victorian font.   HFJP

The doorway high up in the wall above the pulpit once led to the rood loft.   HFJP

The 15th-century font.   HFJP

Note the unusual position of the tower, attached to the S.E. corner of the nave.
HFJP

The church stands well on a hillock above the village, in a raised and partly circular churchyard – usually a sign of antiquity. A visitor approaching from the western gate, seeing the over-excited decoration of the west wall of the church and the wildly extravagant south porch, may well exclaim "Ah! Kempson at it again!", but he would be wrong, for the neo-Norman fantasist at Pencombe is William Nicholson of Hereford. What he did when he rebuilt the church in 1864/5 is interesting. John Leonard notes that that redoubtable Victorian church-crawler Sir Stephen Gwynne saw here in 1856 a church "of mixed Norman and Early English features, and the chancel remarkable for the division into chancel proper and apse". This is confirmed by a water-colour of 1849 hanging in the church, which shows also that the old tower was in the same unusual position as the new one, attached to the south-east corner of the nave. It is therefore clear that Nicholson's new church followed the same plan as the old, reproducing a spread of styles from the 12th to the 14th century, with the addition of his own exuberant and historically questionable decoration. The interior of the church is in fact impressive – spacious and well-proportioned, with a pleasing vista eastwards through the two successive arches to the apse, like a magnified Kilpeck or Moccas.

Pencombe in 1849.   PC

Nicholson's ornate font.   HFJP

The octagonal font, the only relic of the old church.   HFJP

The only relic of the old church is the simple octagonal font, probably of the 15th century. This was ejected at the restoration and replaced by Nicholson's absurdly pompous and ornate affair at the west end. The old font was later rescued, and until recently sat modestly beside the new one, as if in mute protest at Nicholson's extravagance, but it has recently been moved to a curious position at the south-east corner of the nave.

The mural tablet to Richard Jordan (d. 1832) on the south wall deserves attention. Stephen Guest, in his admirable *Notes for visitors*, tells the story of this and other interesting memorials.

There was formerly a church at Marston Stannett, a few miles to the west. This was a chapelry of Pencombe. The church was demolished in 1957, and it survives only in the official name of the parish – "Pencombe with Marston Stannett".

The interior looking east.   HFJP

37

HFJP

The church stands alone on a windy hill-top with wide views in all directions. The churchyard is circular; this is usually taken as a sign of antiquity, and by the gate is what is believed to be part of a prehistoric "standing stone". The church is surrounded by magnificent yews; the particularly splendid specimen on the north of the nave is reputed to be 1200 years old.

The church is of a common local pattern, with chancel, unaisled nave, and a massive squat western tower covered by a pyramidal roof. VR was heavy, but, as so often in these parts, an elegant Norman doorway and some tiny Norman windows have survived. The church contains one very remarkable object – an

In this simple interior note the striking altar frontal.   HFJP

extremely primitive and massive chair, which is said to have been used by St. Augustine of Canterbury in 603 when he came to meet the Welsh bishops in an attempt to persuade them to accept Roman usages, such as the date of Easter. Tradition says that Augustine received the bishops seated in this chair, and discourteously failed to rise to greet them. The bishops took offence at this, broke off the discussion, and returned

The chair said to have been used by St. Augustine when he came to meet the Welsh bishops in 603. HFJP

to Wales with no agreement having been reached. Whether or not this is the actual chair is a matter of opinion. At one time it was in a museum in Canterbury, and its return to Stanford Bishop is described on a brass plate fixed to the chair in such a position that you can only read it if you are prepared to lie flat on your face on the floor holding a torch in one hand. There was a venerable parish chest, but this was regrettably stolen in 1998. The striking altar frontal was designed and made by Elizabeth Hunter – then a parishioner – in the 1970s; the decoration includes a spray of hops and a scallop shell – the emblem of St. James. The long embroidered kneeler at the communion rail was a community effort by a number of local ladies. On leaving the church, notice the enigmatic carved head looking at you over the top of the door.

The Chapel of Ease or Mission Church at Linley Green is a pleasing and dignified little brick building of 1893. The striking and unusual windows are of a geometrical design in red and clear glass, while the dado round the walls was made from the box-pews taken out of Stanford Bishop Church.

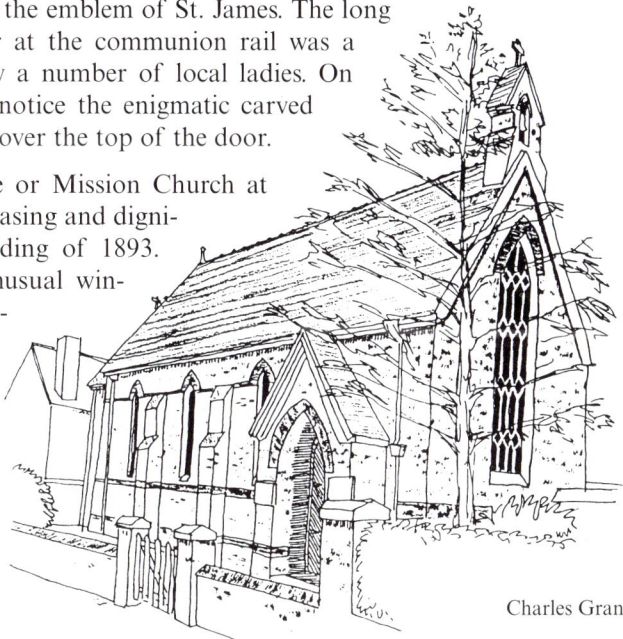

Charles Grant

HFJP

The church appears from the outside to be an entirely Victorian building, and not a very attractive one at that. The "rock-faced" finish of the walls is harsh, and Pevsner unkindly describes the tower and spire as "especially ugly". This is the work of F. R. Kempson in 1863, and here we find him on his home ground, for his father was rector of Stoke Lacy and has a memorial in the church. All that he left of the old church building is the plain Norman chancel arch, and this appears to have been reset and possibly recut. The handsome medieval carved screen in front of it obviously does not fit its present position; one wonders whether Kempson brought it in from some other church that he was "restoring". There is also a nondescript font of uncertain date. On the whole Kempson's handiwork in this church is restrained; only in the over-elaborate piscina and the peculiar pulpit has he let himself go.

The church has an unusually fine collection of 18th- and early 19th-century mural monuments spread around the walls. That to Jane Lilly (d. 1834) on the north wall of the chancel suggests that she was a remarkable and formidable woman. The memorial to her husband the Archdeacon, who sounds rather jollier, was relegated to a place

An aerial view of the church and its surroundings taken in 1947/48. B&DLHS

under the tower, but a recent scheme to convert this area to kitchen, vestry, etc. has entailed moving the Archdeacon to a more visible position on the nave wall.

In the north wall of the nave is a colourful modern window picturing the two saints to whom the church is dedicated; this was installed as a memorial to Hilda Morgan (d. 1956). In the porch is an even more modern one which surprisingly depicts two Morgan cars. This commemorates an American couple who came to Stoke Lacy to attend a Morgan rally in 1995 and fell in love with the place. Sadly they were shortly afterwards killed in a car accident; they left a generous legacy to the church.

This modern window depicting SS Peter and Paul is a memorial to Hilda Morgan (d.1956).
HFJP

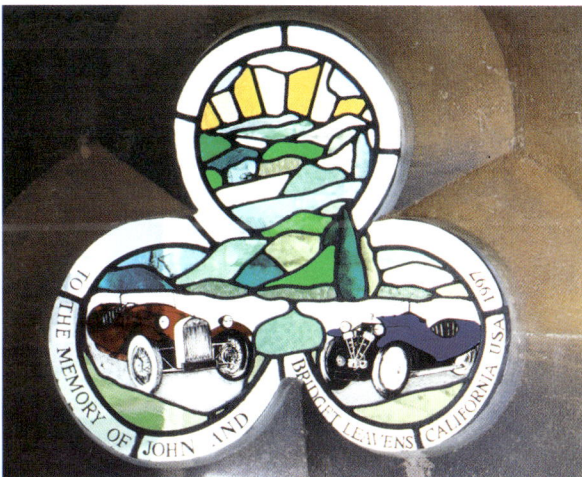

This window is a memorial to an American couple who were both benefactors of the church and Morgan car enthusiasts.
HFJP

TEDSTONE DELAMERE - St. James

HFJP

The church is delightfully situated in the middle of the park of Tedstone Court, some way from the nearest road. As you walk along the path towards it, there is a superb view – particularly in the early evening – over the Severn valley to the Cotswolds. In the spring the churchyard is awash with daffodils; on the left as you enter by the lych-gate, an 18th-century chest-tomb topped by an urn and backed by a dark yew form a picturesque composition. In spite of the heavy VR (see p.4) the little church still shows some bits of Norman (and possibly even earlier) work in the curiously spongy-looking stone called tufa, of which the Norman builders seem to have been fond (see Glossary).

Inside, the church looks entirely Victorian, but a few older relics remain - a (restored) wooden chancel-screen, and a plain, ancient font. This must have been ejected at the restoration in 1856 and replaced by a fancy Victorian one; it has now been brought back, and stands humbly beside its grander brother. The east window is by Hardman; he was one of the greatest 19th-century stained-glass makers - to see how great, one should look at the magnificent east and west windows of Worcester Cathedral, or the even finer glass in the apse of St. Michael's Church, near Tenbury. The harsh and strident colours of this window at Tedstone must surely be attributed to Hardman's workshop, rather than the master himself.

Another noted designer of rather later date, C. E. Kempe, is represented by the much milder window in the north wall of the nave. This shows St. John the Evangelist and his brother St. James, to whom the church is dedicated. He was beheaded by Herod Agrippa in 42 A.D.,

The church in 1850 before its restoration.   B&DLHS

but according to tradition his body was miraculously conveyed in a boat without sails or rudder to the north-east coast of Spain, where his shrine at Compostela became one of the most famous places of pilgrimage in Christendom. St. James is often illogically represented - as in this window - dressed as a pilgrim, with staff, leather bag, and scallop-shell in his hat, though he was of course the object of pilgrimages, not a pilgrim himself.

The two fonts standing side by side. HFJP

In the porch, on the left of the door, is an iron bracket fixed to the wall. This dates back to the 18th or even 17th century, and held an hour-glass beside the pulpit, to time the sermon; its removal to the porch is utterly pointless. Outside the porch, on the left as you leave the church, are the base and shaft of the medieval churchyard cross, topped by a later (1679) sundial and an even later crosshead. The original crosshead (14th-century), sadly weathered, is now preserved in a glazed case set in the wall beside the lych-gate: on one side can just be seen a Virgin and Child and on the other a crucifix. On the opposite side of the path from the cross-base lie two ancient (13th-century?) stone coffin-lids, which must at one time

The east window. HFJP

have been inside the church. They are much worn and covered with grass and moss, but one can just make out a man's face on each.

Altogether Tedstone Delamere is a most attractive place, and in the days when it was a separate parish, the rector must have had an enviable life – as is suggested by a brass in the chancel to Charles Williams, Rector for 42 years (1897-1939). The parishioners who erected the memorial, added as an epitaph the well-chosen text "Be ye steadfast, unmoveable"!

The interior showing the restored chancel-screen. HFJP

Much Cowarne in 1850.   PS

Stoke Lacy in 1850.   PC

Little Cowarne in 1850.   PC

TEDSTONE WAFRE - Old church St. Mary; new church St. James

The chancel screen and pulpit reset in the garden. HFJP

The scanty remains of the medieval church stand in an orchard of magnificent cherry trees some way from the road. Nearby is its replacement, built in 1873. This is a steep-roofed little building of no architectural distinction, though its tall bell-turret forms a landmark for miles around. After standing unused for a number of years it was converted into a private house in 1989.

HFJP

The approach to the church from the south, with Church House Farm to the left.
HFJP

An unusual dedication; St. Anna (or Anne) was the mother of the Blessed Virgin Mary, and in stained glass windows and pictures is usually shown (though not here) seated and holding a book, while her little daughter Mary stands by her knee, learning to read. The approach to the church from the south is dramatic, with the massive fortress-like pyramid-capped tower dominating the little church, while the tower in turn is overtopped by two soaring wellingtonias. To the left is the delightfully prim and formal facade of Church House Farm, a text-book pattern of 18th-century design, complete with forecourt and ball-topped piers.

In spite of drastic VR, three signs of the church's Norman past remain – the font with a carved border, a doorway with typical

An early postcard showing the former spire.
B&DLHS

zig-zag carving on the north side of the church (now blocked), and beside it a tiny round-headed window with a wide inner splay. At one time the church had a south aisle or chapel, and the pillars and arches can be seen embedded in the south wall. The Victorian rebuilding of the chancel regrettably involved the removal of some fine mural monuments to the base of the tower. The Commandments Board (see Acton Beauchamp) which must have been on the

The set of four boards carrying the Ten Commandments, the Lord's Prayer and the Creed.   HFJP

old east wall was at least preserved, and now hangs on the north wall of the nave.

An early postcard shows the tower surmounted by a peculiar timber spire in two stages separated by a decorated vertical section. This is said to have been erected in 1886 and removed in the 1950s, when it was replaced by the present pyramidal roof.

The tiny Norman window.   HFJP

The Norman font.   HFJP

ULLINGSWICK - St. Luke

The church stands in a beautiful and remote situation away from the village, but is neighboured by two fine old farmhouses and a huge Victorian vicarage. The dedication to St. Luke is modern. VR by Kempson in 1862/3 was heavy here, though he left the usual evidence of an older church – two little Norman windows, a nondescript medieval font, and a handsome piscina. He must be given credit for the attractive bell-turret. At the top of the east window is a beautiful panel of the Virgin and Child said to date from the 15th century – but if so, it is much restored. The stonework of this window – it does not deserve the term 'tracery' – is of that basic and boring design which is unfortunately so common in the county that in architectural circles it is known as the "Herefordshire window": we deserve something better. On the north side of the altar is the 13th-century coffin-lid of a priest, carved with a large cross, a chalice and a book. The odd thing is that it was brutally reused for another burial in 1699, as the carved date at the top shows. On the south wall of the nave is a very unusual painted monument to John Hill (d. 1591) representing him lying, richly robed, on a grand tomb-chest, surrounded by his kneeling wife and three surviving children, together with two pathetic little white bundles labelled "John thir sonne" and "Jane thir doughter", who must have both died at birth or in infancy. This seems an ingenious and economical way to achieve the dignity of a tomb-chest without the expense. There are a handsome screen, lectern and pulpit of 1904/5. After the Second World War a memorial vestry was built, using material brought from the ruined church at Avenbury.

In the churchyard is a particularly fine yew, and in early spring any gardener visiting the church will be surprised and gladdened by a remarkable display of pink cyclamen in addition to the mandatory snowdrops.

The screen, lectern and pulpit of 1905. HFJP

A Norman window, evidence of an older church. HFJP

49

HFJP

For once, a church in a village – or at least, on the edge of it. The shingled spire in two stages has a pagoda-like effect, and is crowned by an unusual openwork globe in place of a weather-cock. In spite of the usual heavy VR, much Norman work remains. There are two carved doorways, though the north one is now blocked. (One wonders why here, as at Wolferlow, it was thought necessary to have a grand north door when there are no houses on that side of the church). Inside there is a tiny Norman window in the chancel, and – very surprisingly – another elaborately carved arch opening into the tower, with the wild zig-zag decoration of which the Normans were so fond. This is in fact the original chancel-arch, which was moved to the west end during the VR, and replaced by the present wider and higher one. This could have been a gloomy interior because of the shortage of windows in the nave, the staining of the ceiling between the rafters, and the dark panelling of the chancel (see p.4), but the effect is fortunately mitigated by the plastered and whitewashed walls. There is an attractive window commemorating Mary and William Holder who died in

1900 and 1907, though the style of glass suggests that this must have been installed at a later date. Hidden by the pews nearby is an arched tomb-recess, unfortunately empty, with a crude and vigorous carved head above it, similar to those at Edwyn Ralph.

The Norman chancel arch, now placed at the west end leading to the tower.　　HFJP

The present wider and higher chancel arch which replaced the Norman one. HFJP

A pleasing feature of this church is the elegance and variety of the epitaphs on the numerous memorial tablets on the walls. The earliest is a brass to Hughe Lea (d.1622) with two edifying verses; then comes Henry Huck (d. 1757) who was "cheerful without levity, honest without reserve, an obedient and dutiful son, the best of brothers and friends"; next come John and Edward Seward (d. 1795/96), two admirable young brothers with every imaginable virtue, who sadly died in their twenties, and finally a much-loved Rector, John Walker (d. 1812) whose highly flattering memorial was placed there by his appreciative parishioners. It is regrettable that the 20th century has nothing similar to contribute! Outside the south door are four charming headstones with verse inscriptions, presumably the work of a local poet.

The brass to Hughe Lea. (d.1622).   HFJP

Wacton Church in 1849. PC

The undecipherable ivy-covered stumps of the walls of the ruined church (it was pulled down in 1881) are embedded in a dense thicket next to Wacton Court Farm: a visit is not recommended, except to enthusiasts! An old photograph hanging in Bredenbury Church shows that Wacton Church was a long, low building with a western bell-turret, and what look like two plain Norman doorways and one of the little round-headed windows so often found in local churches. It appears to have been in a derelict condition. When the parishes were united and the church largely demolished in 1881 a set of 17th-century plate from Wacton was transferred to Bredenbury, as was the font, which can now be seen serving as a flowerpot beside the porch there.

The remains of Wacton church in 1900. B&DLHS

WHITBOURNE - St. John the Baptist

An early postcard showing the church and Court.   B&DLHS

The church is attractively situated next to the Court, a rambling, undistin-guished but pleasant house on the site – still partially moated – of one of the favourite palaces or manors of the bishops of Hereford. With the weathered stone of the tower, the medieval lych-gate, and the surrounding cypresses, the church, particularly when snow has fallen, looks like an old-fashioned Christmas card. VR in 1865 unfortunately did dastardly work here, including disastrous scraping of the interior walls, exposing the rough rubble, but the architect in charge (A. E. Perkins, who was responsible for the first stage of the great restoration of Worcester Cathedral) did at least show some originality in building the arcade to his new aisle, and rebuilding the chancel arch, in stone of various muted colours – buff, grey and plum. Fortunately he did not think it necessary to tidy up the odd arrangement of windows in the south wall, and he left two relics of the Norman church – a carved south doorway and a font; the latter has a band of interlocking stars, and on the south side an indetermi-nate animal which looks like a donkey, but is probably an Agnus Dei (the Lamb of God carrying a cross and a banner) which is the emblem of the church's patron saint. What one cannot forgive Perkins for is the disappearance of the charming bell-cote shown in an old drawing hanging in the church, and the moving of the monuments. There are some handsome 18th-century mural tablets disgracefully hidden away under the tower, while some fine ledger-stones were removed from the chancel floor to make room for the usual Victorian tiles, and used to pave the new organ-chamber and vestry. These include one (1704) to Samuel, son of the famous Colonel Birch who resided at Whitbourne Court, and another to a 17th-century rector. Displayed in a frame on the north wall is a large piece of a medieval (15th-century?) vestment of red velvet, embroidered in gold thread with seraphim and other figures.

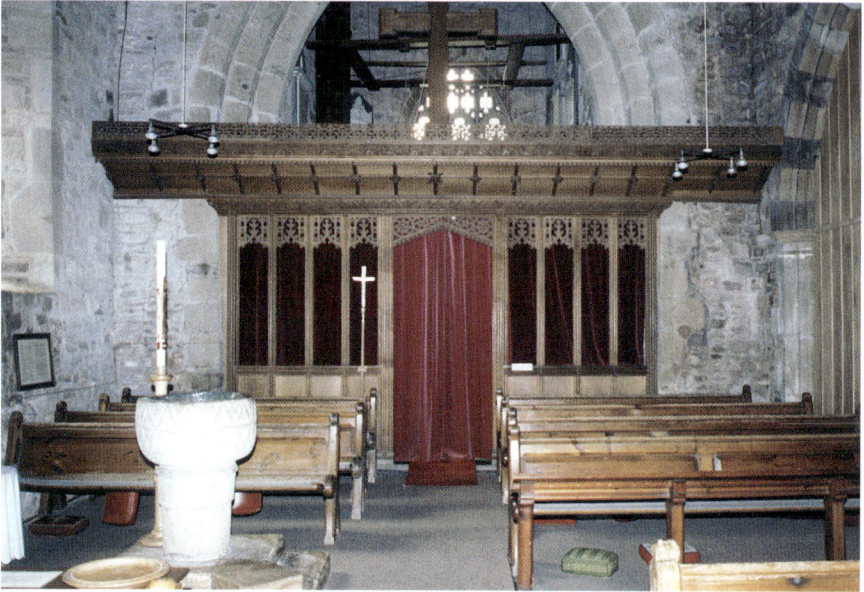

The oak screen now filling the tower arch.   HFJP

The good modern oak screen which stood in the chancel arch has recently (2001) been moved to fill the tower arch at the west end. At the same time the west end of the aisle was enclosed to form a vestry, meeting-room, kitchen, etc.

Behind the altar is a colourful reredos in mosaic set up in 1912: it was made by Powell and Sons, better known for their stained-glass windows. Here the windows are undistinguished, the most pleasing being a little modern one representing St. Francis, unfortunately almost hidden by the clumsy Victorian pulpit. On the south wall is a small brass which must originally have been on a ledger-stone in the floor. Its rather cryptic Latin inscription may perhaps be translated "Hereunder lies Elizabeth, most loving wife of Richard Langford, clerk, and second to his dear Catherine in nothing save in order. She died on 10th February 1708/9 AD aged 32. Together with her lies their son John, died 24th June 1708". If there was once also a brass to the first wife, Catherine, this has disappeared.

The font.   HFJP

54

WHITBOURNE - St. John the Baptist

The mosaic reredos and the "cornfield" embroidered frontal.   HFJP

The curious date 1708/9 is a reminder that in England until 1752 the calendar year used to begin on Lady Day, March 25th, so that dates from 1st January to 24th March were considered as belonging to the previous year. To avoid confusion – for over the rest of Western Europe the year began on 1st January – either the double date was given, as here, or the letters O.S. (old style) or N.S. (new style) added.

Two bishops of Hereford who spent more time at their manor at Whitbourne than at their palace at Hereford were buried in the church. One was Bishop Scory (d. 1584) and the other Bishop Godwin, who died in 1633. One of his books called *The Man on the Moon* is an early attempt at science fiction, in which he foretold human flight and landed his hero on the moon. It is extraordinary and regrettable that no trace of the tombs of either of these bishops remains in the church, though a large plain slab covering what may be Bishop Godwin's tomb came to light when the wooden flooring at the east end of the nave was being removed in 1986.

The medieval lych-gate is roofed with heavy stone tiles, and the old parish bier can be seen stowed under the rafters. Tree-fanciers may like to note on the north side of the church a gingko or maidenhair tree – an unusual tree to find in a churchyard.

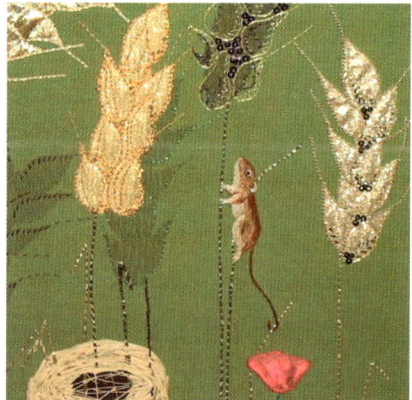

Detail from the frontal, showing a harvest mouse.

HFJP

The church stands in the fields, neighboured to the south-east by the large black-and-white house and farm buildings of Wolferlow Court. The steeple is really a timber-framed tower, carrying the usual shingled spire of this area. Although the top part is modern (19th century) the vast timbers which support it inside the church are centuries older.

The Norman chancel arch with Victorian texts.   HFJP

WOLFERLOW - St. Andrew

Here once again heavy VR has taken its toll, but has left several indications of the Norman origin of the church: there are decorated north and south doorways (the former blocked, the latter simple, but with the round arch oddly filled in) and a plain round chancel arch. The interior is attractively light and contains a great treasure. Under an arched recess in the chancel lies a most beautifully carved stone figure of a lady, dating from the 13th century: she is dressed in a wimple – as nuns used to be until recently – and her mantle is looped over her left arm: at her head two little angels hold back the veil from her face, and at her feet is an animal which one might expect to be a dog, but which looks more like a lion. Her identity is unknown. Sadly, this church is faced with redundancy and is unsafe to enter. The churchyard remains in use as a burial ground.

The 13th-century tomb of an unknown lady.   HFJP

GLOSSARY

APSE	The semi-circular or polygonal end to a chancel or chapel.
ARCADE	A row of arches, particularly those dividing the nave from an aisle.
AUMBRY	A recess or cupboard to hold the sacred vessels used for Mass.
CAPITAL	The carved block on top of a pillar.
CLERESTORY	An upper storey of windows, usually above an aisle to give direct light to the nave.
JAMB	The side of a door or window frame.
LEDGER-STONE	An inscribed grave-slab set into the floor paving.
NORMAN	This term is commonly applied to buildings erected between 1066 and the end of the 12th century. "Norman" work is most easily recognised by the round arch used in the windows, doorways, etc., until gradually ousted by the pointed arch towards the end of the 12th century. The round arch does not reappear in English architecture until the revival of Classical architecture – the Renaissance – in the 17th and 18th centuries. There is therefore a gap of 700 years between the round-arched windows of e.g. Castle Frome (c. 1120) and those of Acton Beauchamp (c. 1820).
PISCINA	A small stone sink with a drain-hole, set in a wall-niche near the altar, for washing the sacred vessels used at Mass.
ROOD, ROOD-LOFT, ROOD-SCREEN	In most medieval churches the chancel was cut off from the nave by a carved wooden screen with double doors in the middle, and window-like openings on either side. The top of the screen projected to the east and west to support a narrow platform – the rood loft – access to which was gained from the chancel by a stone staircase set in the wall. Above the loft a heavy beam supported the rood – a large carved and painted figure of the Crucified Christ, with the Blessed Virgin and St. John on either side. Parts of the service were sometimes said or sung from the rood-loft, and on it candles were lit before the rood. In 1548 Edward VI ordered that all roods should be destroyed, and not a single one survives.
TOMB-CHEST or TABLE-TOMB	A tomb in the form of a rectangular stone box. Until the 18th century these were usually inside the church and carried engraved brasses or carved effigies of those buried beneath. In later times these tombs were placed

GLOSSARY

	in the churchyard, taking a variety of forms, but without an effigy on top.
TUFA	Calcareous tufa or travertine is a spongy-looking but very hard rock formed of the deposit of lime by a spring. This is found in several places in the valleys of the Teme and the Sapey Brook, and was much used in large blocks by the Normans, e.g. at Edvin Loach, Tedstone Delamere and Lower Brockhampton Chapel. A large and dramatic mass of tufa in its natural state can be seen – by those who have the energy to climb up through the woods and find it – at Southstone Rock, high above the Teme downstream from Stanford Bridge. It was very rarely used in church buildings after about 1200.
TYMPANUM	The space between the horizontal lintel of a doorway and the arch above it.

Suggestions for further reading and reference

John Leonard: *Churches of Herefordshire and their Treasures* (Logaston Press 2000).

N. Pevsner: *Herefordshire* in "Buildings of England" series (Penguin 1963).

The following parish histories have been published by the Bromyard and District Local History Society:

AVENBURY Phyllis Williams: *Avenbury and the ruined church of St. Mary* (2000).

BREDENBURY Jennifer Weale: *A History of Bredenbury* (1997).

BROMYARD Phyllis Williams: *Bromyard: Minster, Manor and Town* (1987).

BROMYARD AND STANFORD BISHOP Edna Pearson: *Two churches: two communities* (1993).

LITTLE COWARNE Jean Hopkinson: *Little Cowarne: A Herefordshire Village* (1983).

WHITBOURNE Phyllis Williams: *Whitbourne: A Bishop's Manor* (1979)

All the above books and an extract from the relevant volume of the Royal Commission on Historical Monuments (1931-1934) can be consulted in the research room of the Bromyard and District Local History Society.

St. Peter's Bromyard, the south door.   HFJP